This book belongs to

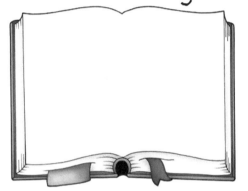

Lily
The Leopard Gecko

Story by Jessica Sterling-Malek
Illustrations by Jason Friend

Dedicated to J.D. & Sasha
For the Great Blue Heron Room

"Mommy, guess What?"

My school said I could bring Lily home for the summer!"

"Who's Lily?" asked Mommy.

"Lily the Lizard!"

"Lily can ride bikes with me!"

"Lily can come to the park with me!"

"Lily can swim with me!"

"Hmmm..." Mommy said. "I don't think Lily can do all those things. Taking care of a pet is a lot of responsibility. I'm not sure this is a good idea."

"PLEASE MOMMY!?
PLEASE MOMMY!?
PLLLEEEEEEEASE!?"

"OKAY," Mommy said. "But, first we should go to the library and learn more about Lizards."

can't read, but Mommy can, so we checked out three ooks about Lizards. I learned a lot more about Lily and ow to take care of her.

learned that Lily is
Leopard Gecko.

Lily is from **this** part of the world.
That's really far from here!

Lily has brown and black spots,
dark eyes, and holes for ears.

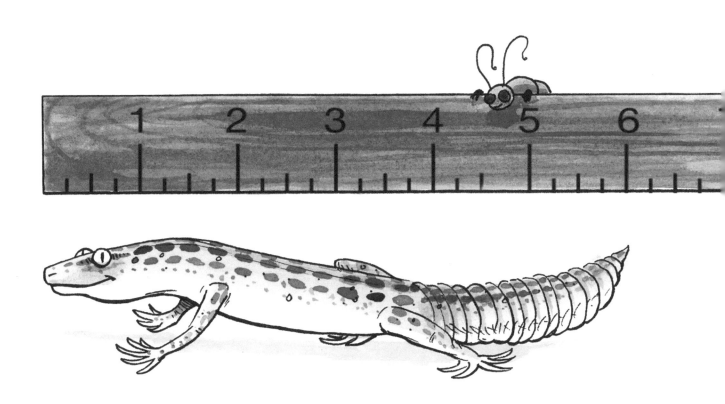

Her fat tail is almost as long as the rest of her body!

"Be careful!
Don't pull her tail
or it might fall off.

"But don't worry, it will grow back!"

Lily is cold blooded, so she needs to live in a very warm
environment. Lily is also nocturnal. That means she
sleeps during the day and is awake during the night.
I will watch over Lily during the day while she sleeps.

And Lily can watch over me at night while I sleep.

Now that I'd learned all about Leopard Geckos,
we went to my school to pick up Lily!

We put Lily in the car.
She rode in the back seat with me.

Teacher Cheryl gave us a list of instructions
to care for Lily during the summer.

Lily Care Instructions

#1 Lily's tank must be heated
#2 Feed Lily live crickets every 2 days
#3 Fill Lily's water bowl every day
#4 Clean Lily's tank once a week

Next, we went to the pet store to buy live crickets for Lily to eat. The pet store worker said that we have to feed the crickets, too.

Crickets eat apples, carrots, and potatoes.

Finally we took Lily home! We set up her tank in my bedroom. When I went to feed her crickets, they all jumped out of their box! There were crickets everywhere!

Daddy was not happy when he found a live cricket in his bed that night!

For the whole summer I played with Lily, filled her water bowl, and cleaned her tank.

Lily grew big, fat, and healthy!
Lily was happy!
Lily is my friend.

Now Summer is over, and it's time to bring Lily back to school. I am sad to see her go, but I am happy to share her again with all my friends at school. I know I will miss her, but I will get to see her every day.

"See you at school tomorrow, Lily!"

CPSIA information can be obtained
at www.ICGtesting.com
Printed in the USA
BVHW021231091121
621118BV00006B/46